PEEK-A-BOO PENGUIN
Ready
for
Reading

Ruth Owen

Consultant: Jillian Harker

QED Publishing

Today, Peek-a-boo Penguin
is visiting a farm.

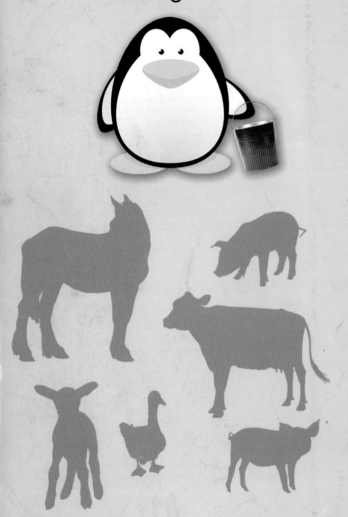

Look at these farm
animal shapes.

Can you match the shapes to the animals in this big picture?

Whose shape is missing?

3

Peek-a-boo is getting ready to go shopping.
It's cold, so he'll need warm clothes.

Can you find Peek-a-boo
two gloves that look the same?

Look for a **pair of socks** that match.
Let's find two **yellow boots**.

Peek-a-boo
is off to town.

Look at the
two pictures.

Do you see
five things
that are
different in
the second
picture?

5

Peek-a-boo has lots to do in town.
He wants to go to the **supermarket**.

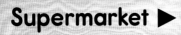
Supermarket ▶

Park ▶

Library ▶

Use your finger to show
Peek-a-boo which
path to take.

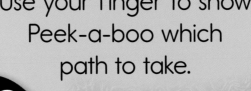

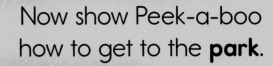

Now show Peek-a-boo
how to get to the **park**.

Help Peek-a-boo
get to the **library**.

Supermarket

Park

Library

Peek-a-boo is at the library.
He's choosing a book to borrow.

Look at the bookshelves.
Can you see a book
on each shelf that is
different to the others?

Peek-a-boo wants something to eat.
What foods does the café sell?

What would you buy for
Peek-a-boo to eat?

Peek-a-boo is shopping in the supermarket.

Can you talk about what he is doing?

Pay here

Look at the supermarket shelves.
One thing looks different
on each shelf.

Point to the thing that is the
odd one out on each shelf.

Peek-a-boo needs some help to pack his shopping.

Look at the pictures on the bags.

BISCUITS

Breakfast crunch

Dog food

Can you show Peek-a-boo which things should go into each bag?

13

Today,
Peek-a-boo
is in the park.

Look at
the pictures.

Can you tell
the story of
Peek-a-boo's
day in the
park?

What do
you think
happens
next?

15

Today, Peek-a-boo is at the safari park.
Look at the two pictures.

There are **10 things** that are
different in the second picture.

How many can you find?

Peek-a-boo is going on holiday.

Can you put the pictures in order
and tell the story of his trip?

Today, Peek-a-boo is at the beach.

Look at all the things that happen at the beach.

Some words are missing from the sentences.
Say the missing words to describe what is happening.

Peek-a-boo is wearing

....

The boat is sailing on the

....

The boy and girl are ....

The children are
.... in the sea.

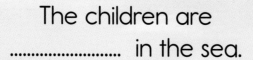

The girl is building a ....

The girl and boy are
playing ....

21

More fun with Peek-a-boo!

Now look back through your book. Let's have some more fun talking about Peek-a-boo's adventures.

Find the pictures that show Peek-a-boo's day in the park. What did Peek-a-boo do at the beginning of his day? What did he do at the end?

Look at the pictures of Peek-a-boo's day at the safari park. Which animals did Peek-a-boo see?

22

Pretend you are having lunch with Peek-a-boo at the café. What would you choose to eat?

Can you think of a day out when you had lots of fun? Tell the story of where you went and all the things you did.

Look through your book. Can you find these things?

Peek-a-boo's house

a tractor

a boat

a plane

Notes for parents and teachers

The activities in this book are designed to introduce children to a range of skills that they will need in order to prepare them for learning to read. The emphasis is on making learning fun, by using an engaging character to capture and focus the interest of young children. The book will help children to develop essential pre-reading skills: matching, observing differences, telling a story in the correct sequence, predicting what might happen next and tracking across a page from left to right.

Sit with the child and read each page to them. Allow time for the child to think about the activity. Encourage them to talk about what they are doing as they carry out the activity. Praise all attempts. If the child is hesitant, show the child how to begin by demonstrating the first part of the activity yourself.

Remember to keep activities short and to make them fun. Stop while your child is still interested. Avoid times when your child is tired or distracted and try another day. Children learn best when they are relaxed and enjoying themselves. It is best to help them to experience new concepts in small steps, rather than to do too much at once.

Use the book as a starting point for activities that your child could carry out at home or when out and about. Some ideas that you could try are:

- Play "Where's Peek-a-boo?" after each activity.

- Encourage your child to retell the events of a day out or a favourite story.

- Allow your child to explore and talk about the illustrations in story books, extracting as much information as possible, before you read the text.

- Pause now and then when reading a story and ask your child to predict what might happen next.

- Play matching games, such as "Snap", using an appropriate set of cards.

Created by: Ruby Tuesday Books
Designers: Elaine Wilkinson and Emma Randall

Copyright © QED Publishing 2011

First published in the UK in 2011 by
QED Publishing
A Quarto Group company
226 City Road
London EC1V 2TT

www.qed-publishing.co.uk

A catalogue record for this book is available from the British Library.

ISBN 978 1 84835 601 6

Printed in China